ICONS

BUENOS AIRES STYLE

BUENOS

Exteriors   Interiors

AIRES STYLE

Details

PHOTOS **Reto Guntli**
EDITOR **Angelika Taschen**

TASCHEN

HONG KONG KÖLN LONDON LOS ANGELES MADRID PARIS TOKYO

Front Cover: Sit on this: old chairs decorate the walls in Ricardo Paz's studio.
Couverture : Les chaises s'envolent : des chai-ses anciennes dé-corent les murs de l'atelier de Ricardo Paz.
Umschlagvorderseite: Nehmen Sie Platz: alte Stühle dekorieren die Wände der Werkstatt von Ricardo Paz.

Back Cover: Walk into blue: an azure-colored door leads to an inner garden.
Dos de couverture : Entrez dans le bleu : une porte couleur d'azur donne sur un jardin intérieur.
Umschlagrückseite: Ins Blaue hinein: eine azurblaue Tür führt in den Innengarten.

Also available from TASCHEN:

The Hotel Book. Great Escapes South America
360 pages
ISBN 978-3-8228-1915-9

To stay informed about upcoming TASCHEN titles, please request our magazine
at www.taschen.com/magazine or write to TASCHEN, Hohenzollernring 53, D-50672 Cologne,
Germany, contact@taschen.com, Fax: +49-221-254919. We will be happy to send you a free copy
of our magazine which is filled with information about all of our books.

© 2008 TASCHEN GmbH
Hohenzollernring 53, D-50672 Köln
www.taschen.com

Concept and editing by Angelika Taschen, Berlin
Layout and general project management by Stephanie Bischoff, Cologne
Texts by Celeste Moure, Buenos Aires
Lithography by Thomas Grell, Cologne
French translation by Philippe Safavi, Paris
German translation by Christiane Burkhardt, Munich

Printed in Italy
ISBN 978-3-8365-0194-1

CONTENTS SOMMAIRE INHALT

A fascinating concoction of politics, history and culture, the sprawling Argentine capital fuses European flair with Latin passion like no other city in South America. With its Neo-Gothic, Neo-Baroque and Renaissance Revival architecture lining its cobblestone streets and the crowds of beautiful people sipping espresso and mastering the art of see-and-be-seen at sidewalk cafés, it's no wonder the city has been likened to Paris, London or Milan. Walk along Avenida de Mayo, the political heart of Argentina, and on one end you'll find the imposing Palacio del Congreso, inspired by the Reichstag in Berlin; at the other end lies Casa Rosada, the presidential palace and the balcony from which Eva Peron once conquered the hearts of the Argentine people. Wander around neighborhoods like San Telmo, with its nostalgic cafés and shady plazas, and La Boca, where tin-roof houses

BUENOS DÍAS

Aucune autre ville d'Amérique du Sud ne marie aussi bien la sophistication européenne à l'ardeur latine que la capitale tentaculaire de l'Argentine, fascinant creuset de politique, d'histoire et de culture. Face à son architecture néogothique, néobaroque et néorenaissance qui borde des rues pavées et à sa population belle à tomber à la renverse qui papote devant des espressos à la terrasse des cafés en peaufinant l'art de voir et d'être vu, on ne doit pas s'étonner si le visiteur songe à Paris, Londres ou Milan. Promenez-vous le long de l'Avenida de Mayo, le cœur politique de la ville, qui part de l'imposant bâtiment du Congrès, inspiré par le Reichstag de Berlin, et va jusqu'à la Casa Rosada, palais présidentiel du balcon duquel Eva Peron a conquis le cœur des Argentins. En flânant dans les quartiers de San Telmo, avec ses vieux cafés et ses places ombragées, et de La Boca, où les maisons au toit en zinc sont peintes de toutes les couleurs de l'arc-en-ciel, vous vous croirez dans une petite ville ouvrière

Mit ihrem faszinierenden Gemisch aus Politik, Geschichte und Kultur verbindet die pulsierende argentinische Hauptstadt europäisches Flair und lateinamerikanische Leidenschaft wie keine andere Stadt Südamerikas. Die kopfsteingepflasterten Straßen werden von Neogotik-, Neobarock- und Neorenaissance-Architektur gesäumt. In den Straßencafés nippen die Schönen und Reichen an ihren Espressos und beherrschen die Kunst des Sehen und Gesehenwerdens meisterhaft. Da überrascht es nicht weiter, dass sich viele Besucher an Paris, London oder Mailand erinnert fühlen. Wer die Avenida de Mayo, das politische Herz des Landes, entlangspaziert, stößt an ihrem Ende auf das imposante Palacio del Congreso, das dem Berliner Reichstag nachempfunden wurde. An ihrem anderen Ende befindet sich die Casa Rosada, der Präsidentenpalast, mit dem berühmten Balkon, von dem aus Eva Peron einst das Herz des argentinischen Volkes eroberte. Erkundet man dagegen Viertel wie San Telmo mit seinen alten Cafés und

are painted in every color of the rainbow, and you'd think you were in a blue-collar Italian town. Elsewhere in the city there are lavish mansions, palaces, train stations and government offices that were financed at the turn of the century by wealthy ranchers and foreign investors and are modeled on iconic European structures. Just a few hours' drive from downtown Buenos Aires you'll come across grand estancias and polo farms, some of which have been passed down from generation to generation. With the economic crisis of 2001 behind them, *porteños*, as the city's inhabitants are called, are now redefining their own style and finding inspiration in their own culture. Like its melancholy national music, the tango, Buenos Aires is a city that hypnotizes at an instant. But, to become better acquainted with the city and to appreciate it fully, you will need to take plenty of time exploring it.

d'Italie. Ailleurs, les hôtels particuliers, les palaces et les bâtiments officiels rappellent des édifices emblématiques d'Europe. Ils furent financés au début du siècle par les investisseurs étrangers et les éleveurs de bétail. A quelques heures de voiture de la capitale s'étendent de somptueux haras et estancias, certains transmis dans la même famille de génération en génération. La crise économique de 2001 étant derrière eux, les porteños, à savoir les habitants de Buenos Aires, redéfinissent aujourd'hui leur style en puisant leur inspiration dans leur propre culture. Comme sa musique nationale mélancolique, le tango, Buenos Aires est une ville qui vous hypnotise sur-le-champ. Mais il faut beaucoup plus de temps pour la comprendre et l'apprécier à sa juste valeur.

schattigen Plätzen oder La Boca, wo es Häuser mit Wellblech-dächern in allen Regenbogenfarben gibt, fühlt man sich beinahe in eine italienische Arbeiterstadt versetzt. Anderswo eifern prächtige Herrenhäuser, Paläste, Bahnhöfe und Regierungsgebäude berühmten europäischen Bauwerken nach. Finanziert wurden sie um 1900 von den Rinderzüchtern und von Ausländern. Von der Innenstadt erreicht man nach nur wenigen Stunden Fahrt jene hochherrschaftlichen Estancias und Polofarmen, die meist schon seit Generationen in Familienbesitz sind. Jetzt, wo die Wirt-schaftskrise von 2001 überwunden scheint, erfinden die *porteños*, wie die Bewohner von Buenos Aires auch genannt werden, ihren Stil neu und lassen sich dabei von ihrer eigenen Kultur inspirieren. Wie die melancholische Nationalmusik, der Tango, zieht auch die Stadt Buenos Aires den Besucher sofort in ihren Bann – doch um sie besser kennen – und richtig schätzen zu lernen, sollte man schon etwas Zeit mitbringen.

"…The urge for good design is the same as the urge to go on living…"

Harry Bertoia

«…Le désir ardent d'une bonne esthétique relève de la même pulsion que le besoin de vivre…»

Harry Bertoia

»…Das Bedürfnis nach gutem Design ist genauso groß wie das Bedürfnis zu überleben…«

Harry Bertoia

EXTERIORS

Extérieurs Aussichten

10/11 Smooth sailing: a ship in Puerto Madero. *Et vogue le navire : un voilier à Puerto Madero.* Ruhig im Hafen: Ein Schiff in Puerto Madero.

12/13 Palacio del Congreso: its Carrara marble steps symbolize the Andes. *Congreso : ses marches en marbre de Carrare symbolisent les Andes.* Palacio del Congreso: seine Stufen aus Carrara-Marmor symbolisieren die Anden.

14/15 Cloudless sky: the fountain on Plaza del Congreso. *Un ciel d'azur : la fontaine de la Plaza del Congreso.* Wolkenloser Himmel: der Brunnen auf dem Plaza del Congreso.

16/17 A moment of quiet: a downtown street in the afternoon. *Un moment de répit : une rue du centre-ville l'après-midi.* Ein Moment der Ruhe: Innenstadtstraße im Nachmittagslicht.

18/19 Flapping in the wind: the national flag flying atop the Congreso. *Bannière au vent : le drapeau national au sommet du Congreso.* Flattern im Wind: die Nationalflagge auf dem Parlamentsgebäude.

20/21 Next stop: colorful buses in a downtown street. *Prochain arrêt : des bus colorés dans une rue du centre-ville.* Nächster Halt: bunte Busse in der Innenstadt.

22/23 Shades of spring: a neighborhood corner market. *Fraîcheur printanière : une épicerie de quartier au coin d'une rue.* Farben des Frühlings: ein kleiner Lebensmittelladen.

24/25 Tropical flavors: fresh fruit at a Palermo Viejo market. *Saveurs tropicales : un étalage de fruits frais sur un marché de Palermo Viejo.* Tropische Genüsse: frisches Obst und Gemüse auf einem Markt in Palermo Viejo.

26/27 Cobblestone streets: a community restaurant in Palermo Viejo. *Rues pavées : un restaurant communautaire à Palermo Viejo.* Kopfsteinpflaster: ein Genossenschaftsrestaurant in Palermo Viejo.

28/29 True colors: the vibrant neighborhood of La Boca. *Haut en couleurs : le quartier pittoresque de La Boca.* Farbe bekennen: bunte Vielfalt in La Boca.

30/31 Lunch special: an outdoor *asado,* or barbecue, in the Province of Buenos Aires. *Plat du jour : un asado (ou barbecue) dans la province de Buenos Aires.* Mittagsimbiss: *asado* oder Grillen im Freien in der Provinz von Buenos Aires.

32/33 Horsing around: an estancia on the outskirts of Buenos Aires. *Chahut chevalin : une estancia dans les faubourgs de Buenos Aires.* Pferde einer Estancia unweit von Buenos Aires.

34/35 Regal standing: a thirsty horse in an estancia. *Port royal : un cheval assoiffé dans une estancia.* Majestätisch: ein durstiges Pferd auf einer Estancia.

36/37 Shady driveway: the entrance to Benquerencia, an estancia. *Allée ombragée : l'entrée de l'estancia Benquerencia.* Schattige Auffahrt: das Eingangstor der Estancia Benquerencia.

38/39 In bloom: the Benquerencia estancia's garden on a summer day. *Floraison : le jardin de l'estancia Benquerencia en été.* In voller Blüte: Der Garten der Estancia Benquerencia an einem Sommertag.

40/41 Colonial times: the stables at the Benquerencia estancia. *Evocation coloniale : l'écurie de l'estancia Benquerencia.* Aus Kolonialzeiten: der Pferdestall der Estancia Benquerencia.

42/43 Strategic planning: polo players exchange a few words. *Mise au point : deux joueurs de polo échangent quelques mots.* Spielstrategie: Polospieler wechseln ein paar Worte.

44/45 Cooling off: waiting for a hose-down after the match. *Rafraîchissement : en attendant la douche après le match.* Erfrischend: Nach dem Match wartet die Dusche.

46/47 Another era: a vintage carriage at the Benquerencia estancia. *Un autre temps : une voiture ancienne dans l'estancia Benquerencia.* Aus einer anderen Ära: eine alte Kutsche auf der Estancia Benquerencia.

48/49 Think pink: Alicia Goni's cheerful polo farm in Pilar. *La vie en rose : le joyeux haras d'Alicia Goni à Pilar.* »Think pink«: Alicia Gonis Polofarm in Pilar.

50/51 Lounging around: creature comforts at Alicia Goni's polo farm. *Doux farniente : la douceur de vivre au haras.* Tierisch bequem: Lounge-Feeling auf Alicias Polofarm.

52/53 No parking: an empty vintage truck at Alicia Goni's farm. *Voie de garage : un vieux camion abandonné dans la ferme d'Alicia Goni.* Parken verboten: ein Oldtimer auf der Farm von Alicia Goni.

54/55 Cat nap: Alicia's cat takes a siesta in the garden. *Heure féline : le chat d'Alicia faisant sa sieste dans le jardin.* Mittagspause: Alicias Katze hält Siesta im Garten.

56/57 Bucolic haven: horses out to pasture at sunset. *Havre bucolique : les chevaux paissant au coucher du soleil.* Bukolisches Idyll: Pferde auf der Weide im Abendrot.

58/59 Crack of dawn: a moment of quiet solitude at sunrise. *Première heure : un moment de solitude paisible à l'aube.* Morgendämmerung: Ungestörtheit bei Sonnenaufgang.

60/61 Lucky break: Alicia Goni on a leisurely ride. *Promenade groupée : la ballade d'Alicia Goni.* Ein glücklicher Zufall: Alicia Goni beim Ausreiten.

62/63 Reflections: the indoors meet the outdoors at La Escondida. *Reflets : l'intérieur et l'extérieur fusionnent à La Escondida.* Spiegelungen: fließender Übergang zwischen drinnen und draußen auf La Escondida.

64/65 Time for a dip: the pool at Fernando de las Carreras' polo farm. *Piquer une tête : la piscine du haras de Fernando de las Carreras.* Zeit zum Planschen: der Pool auf der Polofarm von Fernando de las Carreras.

"…Color does not add a pleasant quality to design – it reinforces it…"

Pierre Bonnard

«…La couleur n'ajoute pas une qualité agréable à l'esthétique, elle la renforce…»

Pierre Bonnard

»…Farbe macht das Design nicht gefälliger, sondern überhöht es…«

Pierre Bonnard

INTERIORS

Intérieurs Einsichten

ARGENTINA ¿Puerta al sur?

ORO EN EL PERU

72/73 Neoclassical elegance: an entrance hall of a French-style apartment building. *Elégance néoclassique : le hall d'un immeuble d'appartements à la française.* Neoklassizistische Eleganz: Eingangshalle in einem Wohnhaus französischen Stils.

74/75 Luminosity: white-on-white simplicity at the Landini's. *Luminosité : simplicité du blanc sur blanc chez les Landini.* Leuchtkraft: Schlichte Weißtöne bei den Landinis.

76/77 Sparkling: a chandelier hangs in the Landini's dining room. *Etincelant : un lustre dans la salle à manger des Landini.* Funkelnder Kristall: der Kronleuchter im Esszimmer der Landinis.

78/79 Flying objects: Fabrizio Clerici's paintings hang in the living room. *Objets volants : des toiles de Fabrizio Clerici dans le séjour.* Flugobjekte: Gemälde von Fabrizio Clerici im Wohnzimmer.

80/81 Golden aura: Joan Bennasar's "Marinero de verano" in Landini's house. *Lumière dorée : « Marinero de Verano » de Joan Bennasar dans le salon des Landini.* Goldenes Licht: Joan Bennasars »Marinero de verano« im Haus der Landinis.

82/83 Bygone days: dusty wine bottles and graffiti at Plaza Dorrego Bar. *Le temps s'est arrêté : bouteilles poussiéreuses et graffitis au bar Plaza Dorrego.* Zeugen der Vergangenheit: verstaubte Weinflaschen in der Plaza-Dorrego-Bar.

84/85 Made to order: maid uniforms adorn a shop window. *Bonne à tout faire : des uniformes de soubrettes dans une vitrine.* »Sie wünschen?«: Serviertrachten in einem Schaufenster.

86/87 Quite a collection: antiques and mementos at artist Gustavo Godoy's. *Soif de collection : antiquités et souvenirs chez l'artiste Gustavo Godoy.* Stolze Sammlung: Trödel und Antiquitäten beim Künstler Gustavo Godoy.

88/89 Long live the queen: the living room at Godoy's studio. *Vive la Reine : le coin salon de l'atelier de l'artiste Godoy.* Lang lebe die Königin: der Wohnbereich in der Werkstatt des Künstlers Godoy.

90/91 Framework: blue walls and vintage frames adorn Godoy's bedroom. *Bien encadré : murs bleus et cadres anciens dans la chambre de Godoy.* Der richtige Rahmen: blaue Wände und alte Bilder schmücken Godoys Schlafzimmer.

92/93 Kiwi and peach: pastels and plants brighten up a room. *Kiwi et pêche : des tons pastel et des plantes égayent la pièce.* Kiwi und Pfirsich: Pastellfarben und Pflanzen bringen den Raum zum Strahlen.

94/95 Fit for a prince: period furnishings in Godoy's San Telmo home. *Décor princier : meubles et tissus anciens dans la demeure de Godoy à San Telmo.* Prinzenwürdig: Historische Möbel in Godoys Wohnung in San Telmo.

96/97 Snack time: on the balcony at Marcelo Lucini's apartment. *Collation : sur le balcon de l'appartement de Marcelo Lucini.* Zeit für einen kleinen Imbiss: auf dem Balkon von Marcelo Lucini.

98/99 Retro modern: vintage chrome lamp in Lucini's lilac dining room. *Rétro moderne : un lustre chromé vintage dans la salle à manger lilas de Lucini.* Retro trifft Moderne: Chromlampe in Lucinis lila Esszimmer.

100/101 Clean lines: art by Pablo Siquier hangs in the living room. *Lignes pures : une œuvre de Pablo Siquier dans le séjour.* Klare Linien: Kunst von Pablo Siquier im Wohnzimmer.

102/103 Minimalist affair: shades of black and white in Lucini's bedroom. *Repos minimaliste : des tons noirs et blancs dans la chambre de Lucini.* Minimalistisch: Schwarz-Weiß-Töne in Lucinis Schlafzimmer.

104/105 Oval window: a delicate linen curtain flows in the wind. *Œil-de-bœuf : un délicat rideau en lin vole au vent.* Fensteroval: Eine zarte Leinengardine flattert im Wind.

106/107 Blown glass: colorful bottles embellish Guereño's cupola apartment. *Verre soufflé : des bouteilles de couleur embellissent l'appartement coupole de Guereño.* Mundgeblasen: bunte Glasflaschen schmücken Guereños Wohnung, die sich in einer Kuppel befindet.

108/109 Stairway to heaven: a spiral staircase leads to Guereño's cupola chill-out space. *Un escalier vers le paradis : un escalier en colimaçon mène au coin repos de Guereño dans la coupole.* »Stairway to heaven«: eine Wendeltreppe führt zu Guereños Chill-out-Space in der Kuppel.

110/111 True colors: bookshelves lined with Asian art in Ed Shaw's apartment. *Couleurs primaires : une bibliothèque accueillant des objets d'art asiatiques dans l'appartement d'Ed Shaw.* Bunte Pracht: Bücherregale mit asiatischer Kunst in Ed Shaws Wohnung.

112/113 Splash of red: a staircase rises up amid masks and statues. *Une touche de rouge : un escalier émerge parmi les masques et les statues.* Roter Farbakzent: Eine Treppe schraubt sich zwischen den Masken und Statuen empor.

114/115 Equine love: horses are omnipresent on Alicia Goni's polo farm. *Amour équin : dans le haras d'Alicia Goni, les chevaux sont partout.* Geliebtes Pferd: Auf Alicia Gonis Polofarm trifft man die Tiere überall.

116/117 Isn't it romantic: an antique fireplace at the polo farm in Pilar. *Romantisme absolu : une antique cheminée dans le haras à Pilar.* Romantik pur: ein antiker Kamin auf der Polofarm in Pilar.

118/119 Hat therapy: straw hats decorate the white bedroom wall in Pilar. *Chapeau ! : des canotiers décorent la chambre blanche à Pilar.* Hut-Tick: Strohhüte dekorieren die Schlafzimmerwand in Pilar.

120/121 Wooden heirloom: Ricardo Paz's handmade chairs and tables. *L'art de la chaise : les sièges et les tables de Ricardo Paz.* Erbstücke aus Holz: Handgeschreinerte Stühle und Tische von Ricardo Paz.

122/123 Timber time: slabs of wood await their future in Paz's warehouse. *Univers ligneux : de vieilles planches attendent leur nouvelle vie dans l'entrepôt de Paz.* Zeit zum Zimmern: Holz, das bald eine neue Zukunft bekommt, in Paz' Lagerhaus.

124/125 Wooden horse: Paz's colorful ponchos and blankets hang on display. *Cheval de bois : les ponchos et les couvertures colorés de Paz.* Holzgerüst: Hier werden Paz' bunte Ponchos und Decken ausgestellt.

126/127 Ready to cook: a simple kitchen at Fernando de las Carreras' estate. *Prêt à cuisiner : une cuisine dépouillée chez Fernando de las Carreras.* »Ready to cook«: eine schlichte Küche auf dem Anwesen von Fernando de los Carreras.

128/129 Beamed in: wooden beams and neutral colors in the living room. *La chaleur du bois : poutres apparentes et tons neutres dans le séjour.* Statik und Ästhetik: Holzbalken und neutrale Farben im Wohnzimmer.

130/131 Think pink: crimson and golden accents at the Benquerencia estancia. *Décor acidulé : des touches cramoisies et dorées dans l'estancia Benquerencia.* Rosarote Zeiten: rote und goldene Akzente auf der Estancia Benquerencia.

132/133 Into blue: azure patterned tiles and ironwork at Benquerencia. *Les tons bleus : azulejos ornés et fer forgé dans l'estancia Benquerencia.* Ins Blaue hinein: azurblau gemusterte Fliesen und Kunstschmiedearbeiten auf Benquerencia.

134/135 Hand-carved dreams: an elegant bed and dresser in the bedroom. *Des rêves sculptés : un lit et une commode superbes dans la chambre.* Handgeschnitzte Träume: ein elegantes Bett samt Kommode.

"…The details are not the details. They make the design…"

Charles Eames

«…Les détails ne sont pas un détail. Ils font le design…»

Charles Eames

»…Details sind keine Details. Sie bestimmen das Design…«

Charles Eames

DETAILS

Détails Details

142 Taking notes: an iconic bar on San Telmo square. *Prenant des notes : un bistrot typique sur la place San Telmo.* Notiert: malerische Bar im San-Telmo-Viertel.

144 Before closing: tomatoes and eggs for sale at a neighborhood market. *Ici, on brade : dans une épicerie de quartier, les tomates et les œufs sont en solde.* Kurz vor Ladenschluss: Tante-Emma-Laden mit Tomaten und Eiern im Angebot.

145 Nostalgic keepsake: book, map and other memories of a distant past. *Rétro souvenirs : un livre, une carte et d'autres souvenirs d'un passé lointain.* Nostalgische Andenken: Buch, Karte und andere Erinnerungsstücke.

146 Rooftop garden: a sunny patio at Teresa Guereño's cupola apartment. *Jardin suspendu : un patio ensoleillé dans l'appartement coupole de Teresa Guereño.* Dachgarten: sonniger Patio vor Teresa Guereños Wohnung.

148 It takes two to tango: a sultry dance on a hot summer day. *Pas de deux : un tango langoureux par une chaude journée d'été.* »It Takes Two To Tango«: temperamentvolle Tänzer an einem heißen Sommertag.

149 Water sports: the Argentine yacht club. *Sport nautique : le yacht club argentin.* Wassersport: der Argentinische Jachtklub.

150 Healthy living: a shop for all things macrobiotic and vegetarian. *La vie saine : une boutique pour les végétariens et les adeptes de produits bio.* Gesund leben: ein Laden mit makrobiotischen und vegetarischen Produkten.

153 Keeping guard: a colorful viewpoint on a bridge. *Sentinelle : une guérite colorée sur un pont.* Alles im Blick: Frohe Aussichten von einer Brücke.

154 A suitable location: Gustavo Godoy's tokens and souvenirs. *Autel domestique : les bibelots et souvenirs de Gustavo Godoy.* Pflichtbesuch: Gustavo Godoys Trödel und Souvenirs.

156 Someone to watch over me: crosses and portraits in Godoy's bedroom. *Sommeil protégé : des portraits et des croix dans la chambre de Godoy.* Ahnen bewachen den Schlaf: Kruzifixe und Porträts in Godoys Schlafzimmer.

157 In the frame: walls filled with art in Godoy's studio. *Bien cadré : des murs tapissés d'œuvres d'art dans l'atelier de Godoy.* Immer im Bild: Wände voller Kunst in Godoys Werkstatt.

158 Gazing heavenward: a Baroque statue in Godoy's living room. *Les yeux au ciel : une sainte baroque dans le séjour de Godoy.* Der Blick geht himmelwärts: eine Barockstatue in Godoys Wohnzimmer.

160 Walk into blue: an azure-colored door leads to an inner garden. *Entrez dans le bleu : une porte couleur d'azur donne sur un jardin intérieur.* Ins Blaue hinein: eine azurblaue Tür führt in den Innengarten.

161 Royal tendencies: a statue on stacks of paper in Godoy's studio. *Royale sainteté : une statue sur une pile de vieux papiers dans l'atelier de Godoy.* Wahrhaft königlich: Statue auf Papierstapel in Godoys Werkstatt.

162 Luminescence: bright light through an oval window in Guereño's cupola. *Luminescence : une fenêtre arrondie dans la coupole de Guereño.* Leuchtkraft: Sonnenlicht, das durch ein ovales Fenster in Guereños Kuppel fällt.

164 Tiny steps: a spiral staircase leads to Guereño's chill-out space. *A petits pas : un escalier en colimaçon mène au coin repos de Guereño.* Stufe für Stufe: eine Wendeltreppe führt zu Guereños Chill-out-Space hinauf.

165 Rainbow vases: multihued glass bottles in Guereño's studio. *Un arc-en-ciel en verre : des bouteilles multicolores dans l'atelier de Guereño.* Regenbogenvasen: Bunte Glasflaschen in Guereños Werkstatt.

167 Sitting pretty: painting by Noé above vintage chair and table. *Bonne assise : une toile de Noé au-dessus d'une chaise et d'une table vintage.* Perfekt zum Sitzen: Gemälde von Noé über einem Vintage-Stuhl und -Tisch.

168 Avant-garde Lolita: a statue by Martin Di Girolamo at Lucini's house. *Lolita avant-gardiste : une statuette de Martin di Girolamo chez Lucini.* Avantgarde-Lolita: Statue von Martin Di Girolamo im Haus der Lucinis.

169 Richly decorated: candlesticks below an Alfredo Hlito painting in Lucini's house. *Opulence : des bougeoirs devant un tableau d'Alfredo Hlito chez Lucini.* Reich geschmückt: Kerzenhalter unter einem Gemälde von Alfredo Hlito im Haus der Lucinis.

170 Earth tones: a beautifully tiled bathroom in Lucini's house. *Couleurs de terre : une belle salle de bains en mosaïque chez Lucini.* Erdfarben: ein schön gefliestes Bad im Haus der Lucinis.

172 Birds of paradise: a birdhouse on the Goni polo farm. *Oiseaux de paradis : une maisonnette pour les oiseaux au haras Goni.* Paradiesisch: ein Vogelhaus auf der Goni-Polofarm.

173 Basic basket: fruits right off the tree, sitting in the sunshine. *Le panier de la ménagère : des fruits cueillis dans l'arbre attendent au soleil.* Vitaminpaket: Obst direkt vom Baum wartet in der Sonne.

174 Suddenly citrus: a yellow room on the Goni polo farm. *Beauté citrique : une pièce jaune dans le haras Goni.* Zitrusgelb: ein gelbes Zimmer auf der Goni-Polofarm.

176 Learning to ride: a young kid bonds with his new friend at the farm. *Les bases de l'équitation : un enfant fait connaissance avec son nouvel ami.* Reiten lernen: ein Kind mit seinem neuen Freund auf der Farm.

177 After the match: riding boots and polo gear. *Après le match : des bottes et un équipement de polo.* Nach dem Match: Reitstiefel und Poloausrüstung.

178 Hanging matters: mallets at the Goni polo farm. *En suspens : des maillets de polo au haras Goni.* Ordentlich verstaut: Schläger auf der Goni-Polofarm.

180 Making a statement: an antique armoire at Fernando de las Carreras'. *Imposante : une armoire ancienne chez Fernando de las Carreras.* Imposant: eine Schrankbar auf dem Anwesen von Fernando de los Carreras.

181 Hungry times: a tasty *asado* awaits the polo players. *Un petit creux : un succulent asado attend les joueurs de polo.* Für Ausgehungerte: Auf die Polospieler wartet ein leckeres *asado*.

182 Play me a song: a lonely chair and guitar await a musician. *Joue-moi une chanson : une chaise et une guitare attendent un musicien.* Spiel mir ein Lied: eine einsame Gitarre wartet auf einen Musiker.

184 Sit on this: old chairs decorate the walls in Ricardo Paz's studio. *Les chaises s'envolent : des chaises anciennes décorent les murs de l'atelier de Ricardo Paz.* Nehmen Sie Platz: alte Stühle dekorieren die Wände der Werkstatt von Ricardo Paz.

185 Climbing up the walls: a white door and rickety ladder. *Grimper au mur : une porte blanche et une vieille échelle.* Nur für geübte Kletterer: eine weiße Tür nebst klappriger Leiter.

186 For whom the bell tolls: an iron bell on a white wall at Benquerencia. *Pour qui sonne la cloche : une cloche en fer sur un mur blanc à l'estancia Benquerencia.* Wem die Stunde schlägt: eiserne Glocke vor einer weißen Wand auf Benquerencia.

The Hotel Book.
Great Escapes South America
Ed. Angelika Taschen
Hardcover, 360 pp. / € 29.99 /
$ 39.99 / £ 24.99 / ¥ 5.900

The Hotel Book.
Great Escapes North America
Ed. Angelika Taschen
Hardcover, 400 pp. / € 29.99 /
$ 39.99 / £ 24.99 / ¥ 5.900

The Hotel Book.
Great Escapes Asia
Ed. Angelika Taschen
Hardcover, 400 pp. / € 29.99 /
$ 39.99 / £ 24.99 / ¥ 5.900

"This is one for the coffee table, providing more than enough material for a good drool. Gorgeousness between the cover." —*Time Out,* London, on *Great Escapes Africa*

" Buy them all and add some pleasure to your life."

60s Fashion
Ed. Jim Heimann

70s Fashion
Ed. Jim Heimann

African Style
Ed. Angelika Taschen

Alchemy & Mysticism
Alexander Roob

Architecture Now!
Ed. Philip Jodidio

Art Now
Eds. Burkhard Riemschneider,
Uta Grosenick

Atget's Paris
Ed. Hans Christian Adam

Bamboo Style
Ed. Angelika Taschen

Barcelona,
Restaurants & More
Ed. Angelika Taschen

Barcelona,
Shops & More
Ed. Angelika Taschen

Ingrid Bergman
Ed. Paul Duncan, Scott Eyman

Berlin Style
Ed. Angelika Taschen

Humphrey Bogart
Ed. Paul Duncan, James Ursini

Marlon Brando
Ed. Paul Duncan, F.X. Feeney

Brussels Style
Ed. Angelika Taschen

Cars of the 70s
Ed. Jim Heimann, Tony Thacker

Charlie Chaplin
Ed. Paul Duncan, David
Robinson

China Style
Ed. Angelika Taschen

Christmas
Ed. Jim Heimann, Steven Heller

James Dean
Ed. Paul Duncan, F.X. Feeney

Design Handbook
Charlotte & Peter Fiell

Design for the 21ˢᵗ Century
Eds. Charlotte & Peter Fiell

Design of the 20ᵗʰ Century
Eds. Charlotte & Peter Fiell

Devils
Gilles Néret

Marlene Dietrich
Ed. Paul Duncan, James Ursini

Robert Doisneau
Ed. Jean-Claude Gautrand

East German Design
Ralf Ulrich/Photos: Ernst Hedler

Clint Eastwood
Ed. Paul Duncan, Douglas
Keesey

Egypt Style
Ed. Angelika Taschen

Encyclopaedia Anatomica
Ed. Museo La Specola Florence

M.C. Escher

Fashion
Ed. The Kyoto Costume Institute

Fashion Now!
Eds. Terry Jones, Susie Rushton

Fruit
Ed. George Brookshaw,
Uta Pellgrü-Gagel

Greta Garbo
Ed. Paul Duncan, David
Robinson

HR Giger
HR Giger

Grand Tour
Harry Seidler

Cary Grant
Ed. Paul Duncan, F.X. Feeney

Graphic Design
Eds. Charlotte & Peter Fiell

Greece Style
Ed. Angelika Taschen

Halloween
Ed. Jim Heimann, Steven Heller

Havana Style
Ed. Angelika Taschen

Audrey Hepburn
Ed. Paul Duncan, F.X. Feeney

Katharine Hepburn
Ed. Paul Duncan, Alain Silver

Homo Art
Gilles Néret

Hot Rods
Ed. Coco Shinomiya, Tony
Thacker

Grace Kelly
Ed. Paul Duncan, Glenn Hopp

London, Restaurants & More
Ed. Angelika Taschen

London, Shops & More
Ed. Angelika Taschen

London Style
Ed. Angelika Taschen

Marx Brothers
Ed. Paul Duncan, Douglas
Keesey

Steve McQueen
Ed. Paul Duncan, Alain Silver

Mexico Style
Ed. Angelika Taschen

Miami Style
Ed. Angelika Taschen

Minimal Style
Ed. Angelika Taschen

Marilyn Monroe
Ed. Paul Duncan, F.X. Feeney

Morocco Style
Ed. Angelika Taschen

New York Style
Ed. Angelika Taschen

Paris Style
Ed. Angelika Taschen

Penguin
Frans Lanting

Pierre et Gilles
Eric Troncy

Provence Style
Ed. Angelika Taschen

Safari Style
Ed. Angelika Taschen

Seaside Style
Ed. Angelika Taschen

Signs
Ed. Julius Wiedeman

South African Style
Ed. Angelika Taschen

Starck
Philippe Starck

Surfing
Ed. Jim Heimann

Sweden Style
Ed. Angelika Taschen

Tattoos
Ed. Henk Schiffmacher

Tokyo Style
Ed. Angelika Taschen

Tuscany Style
Ed. Angelika Taschen

Valentines
Ed. Jim Heimann, Steven Heller

Web Design:
Best Studios
Ed. Julius Wiedemann

Web Design:
Best Studios 2
Ed. Julius Wiedemann

Web Design:
E-Commerce
Ed. Julius Wiedemann

Web Design: Flash Sites
Ed. Julius Wiedemann

Web Design:
Music Sites
Ed. Julius Wiedemann

Web Design: Portfolios
Ed. Julius Wiedemann

Orson Welles
Ed. Paul Duncan, F.X. Feeney

Women Artists
in the 20th and 21st Century
Ed. Uta Grosenick

ICONS